The
Japanese Garden

Story by Sally O'Neill and Nan O'Neill   Illustrations by Claire Bridge

Nikko and Shari Akira
lived with their parents in California.

Their father often had to go
on business trips to Japan.
While he was away,
they missed him very much.

Every time Mr. Akira came home,
he had photos to show them.
He told Nikko and Shari
about the crowded city in Japan
where he worked.
"Most people have very small houses
and gardens," he said.
"It is hard for you to imagine
just how small these gardens are."

"In Japan there are some people
who never leave the big cities,"
explained Mr. Akira.
"They have to travel a long way
across the city to get to work.
So their peaceful gardens
are very important to them.
Before they leave home each morning,
they like to spend time there."

Nikko and Shari loved to hear
about the tiny gardens.
They imagined the things inside them:
the rocks, the water, the pebbles,
the small plants,
and the little stone lanterns.

Mr. Akira showed the children photos
of the little garden at the hotel
where he stayed.
"I often sit in this beautiful place,"
he said.
"I look at the rock and see a mountain.
I listen to the waterfall
and think of a river.
I look at the small bamboo trees
and see a deep forest.
Then I am ready to start work
in the busy city."

"We miss you so much when you are away,"
Nikko said to his father.
"Won't you take us to Japan
next time you go?"

"We'd love to see the little garden
that you sit in," said Shari.

"I'm sorry," said Mr. Akira.
"I can't take you on my business trips."

A few days later,
Mr. Akira went back to Japan.
Nikko and Shari felt very sad.

But Mrs. Akira said to them,
"We could make our own Japanese garden
in the backyard.
Then while your father is away,
we could go there and think of him."

The children loved the idea.
They hurried outside with their mother
and cleared a place in a corner of the yard.
Then they began to plan their garden.

The next day, Mrs. Akira and the children
went to the garden store.

They bought a tall rock, and some stones,
some pebbles, and some soft green moss.

They bought some little trees
and other plants,
and bamboo to make a forest.

They bought a bowl
to hold the sparkling water.

The last thing they bought
was a small stone lantern
to make their garden special.

As soon as they got home,
they planted the bamboo forest.
They put the tall rock in the corner
to make a mountain.
They laid some of the stones around it.

They put the large stones
on the other side of the garden.
They placed the water bowl carefully on top
of the stones.
They put one end of the hose into the bowl,
and it began to fill with water.
They added the green moss
and the rest of the plants.
Then they spread the pebbles.

As the water flowed out of the bowl,
it made a soft splashing noise
just like a mountain stream.

Last of all, they put the lantern
in front of the forest.

They stood back and admired their garden.
It was beautiful.

In the quiet of the early morning,
and again in the evening,
Nikko and Shari sat on the wooden bench
by their Japanese garden.
They listened to the sound of the water
flowing down over the stones,
and they thought of their father in Japan.

When Mr. Akira arrived home
at the end of the week,
Nikko and Shari took him
to see their garden.
He was amazed.
"It's beautiful!" he said.
"It looks just like the garden
at my hotel."

And he put a candle in the lantern.

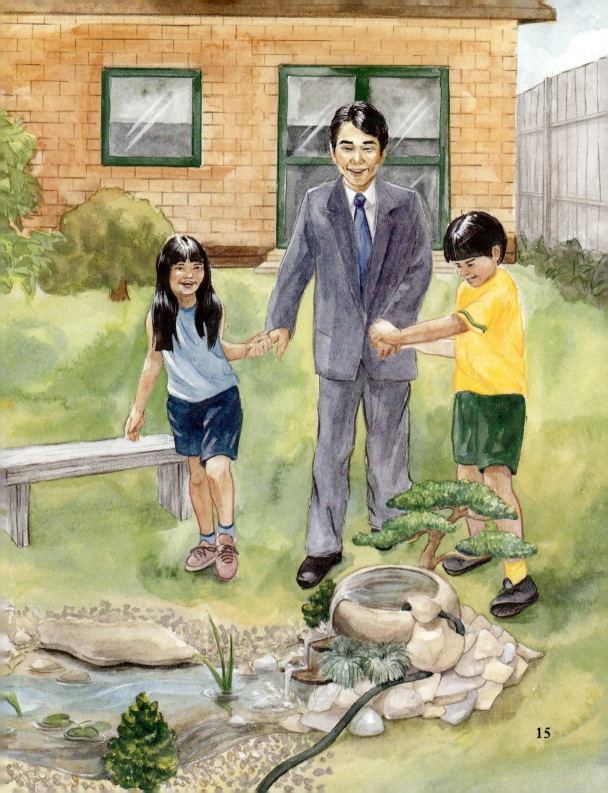

That evening, Mr. Akira lit the candle.
The flickering light made patterns
on the rocks and pebbles.
Nikko and Shari loved their garden.
It was their special place.

"Whenever you are away,
we can sit here and think of you,"
Shari said to her father.

"And you can sit in your Japanese garden
and think of us," said Nikko.